Life According to An Unknown

Todays World Seen Through the Eyes of a Woman

Hillary R. Raimo

Bloomington, IN      Milton Keynes, UK

authorHOUSE®

AuthorHouse™
1663 Liberty Drive, Suite 200
Bloomington, IN 47403
www.authorhouse.com
Phone: 1-800-839-8640

AuthorHouse™ UK Ltd.
500 Avebury Boulevard
Central Milton Keynes, MK9 2BE
www.authorhouse.co.uk
Phone: 08001974150

First published by AuthorHouse 9/28/2006

ISBN: 1-4259-5058-2 (sc)

*Printed in the United States of America
Bloomington, Indiana*

This book is printed on acid-free paper.

For Poppop

Acknowledgements

There are certain people who touch our lives and change it forever. They come and go or stay for awhile. Perhaps even an entire lifetime.

These people cross our paths and forever alter our lives.They change us in ways that allows us to grow into a more whole human being.

Lynn V. Andrews and the Sisterhood of the shields has done just that for me. Their presence in my life has changed me forever. I want to thank Lynn for her guidance and for teaching me the ways of the sisterhood. I am forever grateful.

To all my fellow sisters in LACSAT. My dreaming bear lodge and my beloved writers circle. All of you are forever my spiritual family.

To my dear friend Vicki Dobbs. Your guidance and never ending support has shown me the true meaning of unconditional love. Thank you for always being there for me whenever I needed you and for always believing in me. You are a true friend.

To Pam Gemperle and all our long conversations full of wisdom, and laughter. Thank you for all your insight and friendship along the way.

To Susan Maguire and our ceremony in the desert.

To Gloria Pringle and all the love and support all these years. To Deb Caine and all our amazing letters over all these years, your energy and light has always inspired and touched my heart.

To Peg Hubbard, my friend, roommate and editor. Thank you for all your hard work and believing in this book.

Thank you to my mentor of four years through LACSAT, Rev. Jan Ives. Your amazing presence and support through my years of waking up will never be forgotten.Your humor and love and wisdom are now pillars of strength within me forever. Thank you.

I want to thank my mother Anne Magee for everything we have gone through together. It has deepened and enriched my life in more ways then I can count. I know how much you have loved me all my life, and I honor all that you are forever. I love you deeply and want to thank you for growing with me through all the storms of our relationship. Without you I would not be who I am today. I will always remember our healing journey together in the deserts of Joshua Tree. Thank you Mom for everything.

For my grandmothers Katherine Magee and Miriam Holloway.

For my sister Caitlin and the special bond that holds so much truth between us.

I wish to especially thank Anthony, my husband, for all your patience and support as I struggled with finding myself all these years. I know it has not always been easy. Through all the good times and bad you are my love. The laughter and the tears bring truth to my memories, my heart and to my soul.

Thank you for loving me and supporting me as I manifested my dreams.

Most important to Anthony Jr. and Michael. Two beacons of light from the most brilliant star above. Without you both my life would never be the same. You have taught me the importance of innocence, laughter, play and remind me always never to take life so seriously that you lose sight of what is truly important. I love you both forever.

Finally, for the light and dark side of passion and all the lessons it has shown me.

Note to the Reader

There comes a time in a womans life when you look around at what you have created and reevaluate everything. Your body, your choice of partner, your career, your passions and what it is that you truly want in your life.Some call it a crisis, I call it an awakening.

It takes courage and strength to stand up to what you have already invested so much into and decide whether or not it stays or goes. It is like knowing your death has arrived to take you and you must say goodbye to some very treasured moments in life.

Risk entered my life one day and told me to take a good long look at where I was in my life at that very moment. Challenge came along too and asked me to really look closely at my choices up until then. This can be very healing and also terrifying.

Some things I would have changed and some things I wouldn't.

This book was a product of that searching. Risk and challenge became intimate lovers for me as I traveled through this awakening. They asked me to question everything.To realign what worked in my life with what I wanted and to let go of what didn't.

I looked back on my life much like a recapitulation and sorted through the memories and took the nuggets of gold, the lessons, and choose to see wisdom instead of pain.

I craved connection. Something which had eluded me up until then, maybe it had visited once in awhile, but it was like a wind, it came and went. Never knowing when it would return.I wanted more. I wanted that wind to stay, that connection to fill me and not just visit randomly anymore, but to become a permanent fixture in my life.I wanted more, and in order to get that I needed to change how I saw everything around me.

Change is the one thing we are all so afraid of. Fear became my good enemy, and I choose to take it on and its all powerful control over my life.

This story is the conception and product of the dance and intimate seduction of overcoming my fear to speak the truth, not only to myself, but to others as well.To seek connection without being afraid.To trust my inner guides and my relationship with spirit enough to carry me through the unknown in life. To trust in human nature and believe that connection between one another is possible simply because we are all human.

Listen to another persons story, share your own and learn from one another.

It is perhaps the true meaning of life.

Hillary R. Raimo

Our deepest fear is not that we are inadequate. Our deepest fear is that we are powerful beyond measure. It is our light, not our darkness, that most frightens us. We ask ourselves, who am I to be brilliant, gorgeous, talented, and fabulous? Actually, who are you not to be? You are a child of God. Your playing small doesn't serve the world. There is nothing enlightened about shrinking so that other people will not feel insecure around you. We were born to make manifest the glory of God that is within us. It is not in just some of us; it is in everyone. And as we let our own light shine, we unconsciously give people permission to do the same. As we are liberated from our own fear, our presence automatically liberates others.

- Marianne Williamson, from *A Return to Love*, as quoted by Nelson Mandela in his inaugural speech as president of South Africa, May 1994

Chapter 1

After ten years of marriage, I look around at my life and I'm not sure how I should feel. Part of me wants to run and go cry in the corner for a day or two, in straight fear of what I have become. Another part of me is ready to be here. To settle and make my life all about my kids and my husband. Cleaning my house, when my cleaning lady isn't here anyway, and cooking dinner.

Another part says run like hell.

I hear this stage in life is called a mid life crisis. Maybe it is a crisis. Maybe it is a discovery. Either way doesn't matter, as long as I survive it.

Maybe I will discover who I really am and get a chance to step back and evaluate my life and what

I'm doing with it or more specifically what I am not doing with it.

Isn't it true we all have a great destiny? I have always heard this and wondered WOW.... when will I find mine?

So I look and look. Search some more, read another great self help book, watch another show. Nope not here. Haven't found it yet, but it all tells me to keep looking.

Keep looking.

A lot of good that does. Always on the go to search some more. I traveled to the far ends of the earth looking for it. Never found it. One constant was I always came home to my own home. My family. My husband and kids.

Why is that not enough? A voice still wonders at a subconscious level. Swirling just below the perimeters of the surface of my mind.

What is this thirst? Am I looking for God? As some say, that is what life is all about. I say what about making a living, buying groceries, paying for gas! Now that is a feat in its own right. Gas prices these days make the common blue-collar worker have heart palpitations. Or what about the single mom who can't collect on the dead-beat dad. How do they survive and thrive as human beings.

What about the ordinary everyday world around me. Why don't people look people in the eye anymore. When I walk by someone, there is nothing. No connection. Nothing. Where is it?

There seems to be more connection in the world, with all the new high tech technology. We claim we are creating a greater and greater web. I say it just makes us more and more tangled and less connected to each other in the way that matters.

There is great sadness here. A great void. Where are all the stories? Everyone has one. Everyone has had a tale or two in their life. Where are the listeners?

You as my reader are listening to me. Sharing my story. Listening to my unknown voice in the world.

Who am I to have an opinion? I say I am just like you and we both deserve to hear each other.

My marriage has had its ups and downs. As most do, I suppose.

My husband is a good provider. He works all the time. There are so many times I have felt left out of his life because of it. The more responsibility that comes our way, the more money we make, the older our kids get, the less we do together. A lot of sadness and regret in this department and a lot of anger as well.

Would it be worth finding a lover to fill the holes in my sexual life? To find the spark again? Should I bother trying with someone who has no interest in me? I really am invisible to him. I'm surprised he even remembers my name. I laugh at that, don't feel sorry for me over that. I don't want pity or judgment for my thoughts. Everyone thinks about being with other people. It is human nature. We are sexual beings. Procreation is a natural and built in instinct. It is in our wiring. Maybe that is why the porn industry makes more money then most other industries.

If we can't really go out and do it, then why not just rent a movie, look on the Internet and masturbate? It is easier then getting tangled in the webs of an affair. No emotional investment, no headaches, no one gets hurt and you can still orgasm to the most bizarre fantasies without ever getting caught up in the moral issues of it.

I say good for you if that is your goal. Again what about the emotional investment? The connection? The touch of another body.

Where has that all gone.

And if you do choose to do it, go out and open yourself to the hidden and forbidden world of adultery, what then?

Doesn't make life much easier. Especially when you get emotionally connected. There is never a good ending to that story.

What if we could all look down the trail of our own lives. What would we see, do different? Change, stay away from? What decision would we make sure we changed.

What would be yours?

What things about your life would you have done differently. Would you have said no to the person you married. Would you have said yes to another.

Would you have had the courage to say no to someone, try the drug you've always been afraid of doing. Had sex with that person who was really into you and you turned down.

We have the power within us to do so much. Yet how does one activate that software within. Does one even bother any more. Why bother when you have so much to do outside of yourself. Looking within is boring, and who has the time nowadays?

So much to keep up with; after all, beating your neighbor in the war of who has better stuff really is important!

Or making sure you lose one more dress size so you can fit into that certain dress, now that really matters much more then surfing the interiors of your own coastline! Besides its much safer to bury your mind in the workings of distraction so you don't have to actually change or move.

Why move out of your safety zone for a moment to allow the newness of something different to come in. Let's just keep ourselves blocked and safe behind closed doors so we can know what to expect in life.

That is what antidepressants are for. Or medications of choice, drugs, alcohol, sex.

Let's be addicted to something so we never have to change.

Now isn't that much better then working on your self! Let's do what most Americans do. Point the finger at the other guy. Point out all the faults, problems, and things they should be doing to change their life. Let's fix the other man because that is much easier then fixing ourselves now isn't it.

Someone close once said to me, when you point a finger at another, you have three pointing back at you.

The great tragedy in life is the great fear that circles us to never look within. To never just sit and do nothing. To give our minds a break. We are so afraid to allow that moment to happen, because of what we might actually feel.

That is the true meaning of depression, I think. Keeping safely away from our true feelings so we never feel them. Never give them a voice or a chance to come out.

God forbid we get angry. Or cry. Or tell another we love them.

And mean it. We might melt away into indistinguishable puddles of waste if we were to do that.

Yes, there is some sarcasm there.

I once knew someone special in my life who I loved very much. We should've been together, but both of us were always so afraid of what it would take to actually be a couple. We would have to leave the unhappy relationships we were already in, change our everyday lives and create a new one.

Sounds so simple. Yet it is the scariest thing to someone who is afraid of the unknown in life.

You see, that fear that circles each of us swirls around us like a slight fog, or scent. We keep to our schedules. Worry about tomorrow based on the past. Run around doing.

Never just being. Never letting ourselves show our vulnerability. God forbid someone else sees us as weak.

I laugh and say, "So what! You are no different then I!" We are both human beings.

So few see the beauty in that anymore. When did it become all about beating everyone else at the game of life, when life is really about being together thru the game.

But then again, what do I know? I'm a nobody.

Who cares about the world according to an unknown. You might find something wrong with me, my writing technique, style, maybe even how I have chosen to live my life. I say go ahead. I am no different then you. No better and no worse. Nothing I do is any different then you. I have done all of these things. I have walked by people and never looked them in the eye. Made fun of my waitress when she was old and fat. Hurt others with my words.

It was a choice I had to make one day to stop. To look at another and start seeing. To just look and smile. Know that they are flesh and bone like me. To know that I am not perfect allowed me to see others as imperfect and beautiful at the same time.

A great teacher once said to me that, like a great crystal, the ones that reflect the most beauty and light are the ones with the most cracks. You can't see rainbows if there aren't any cracks. Our cracks are our imperfections. What makes us weak makes us beautiful.

But again, why listen to my words. I am just an unknown. Like you, a voice in the ocean of many. No one cares what I think. Why should they? I have no money, no political influence. I wont be on the Oprah show or on Dr. Phil. I have no fancy letters after my name. I have just raised kids, made snack after school, waited tables to make a living. What do I know about life? You could put this book back on the shelf and keep looking, and I'll never know.

Or you can pull up a chair, settle down and stay awhile. We could share each other's company for a time. Listen. And maybe learn a thing or two.

I'm not trying to change the world. I'm just trying to make a ripple in a small pond. Perhaps so I can find my own salvation.

Or maybe just so I can be heard.

A thirst we all have within us.

Chapter 2

When I worked as a waitress there was a woman who came in everyday. Sat at the same table, always ordered pretty much the same thing. Usually hoped she would have the same waitress. Always had an unsweetened ice tea and a chicken sandwich. I usually got her, as I was one of the "day girls".

In the beginning when she first started coming in, I would be annoyed she was here, because she wasn't a very good tipper, she would take up my table for an hour, and leave me two dollars.

A tragedy in the world of waiters and waitresses!

Very few people seem to be aware that we were only paid $3.90 an hour on the average. That we all lived off our tips and some of us had families to support or school to pay for.

Hopes and dreams to fund.

Many people took much satisfaction in tipping as little as possible. Run us around; ask for sides of things every time we came back to the table. All the time knowing we had to be nice, or they would just ask for the manger, complain and know our jobs would be at stake. And I must say in the world of corporate restaurants, they are much more concerned about the guest then their staff. If many knew how waiters and waitress were treated behind the scene of "all is well in our establishment" they would never spend a dime in that place again. In my opinion all corporate restaurants treat their employees like slaves. And we were all replaceable.

I began to look forward to her visits. Her strict routine of life. I found it comforting at times. I knew her and she knew me. The holidays came around and she sent a gift to me and another woman who she had as her server often. She was polite, and always seemed happy with life.

One day her table was taken as she came in for her lunch. She had to sit somewhere else. Everyone there that day knew she was mad. She made it very clear.

We never saw her again.

What is it about the routine of life that we find so safe. Who says everything is as it should be. What if they are wrong? What if everything is the way it is only because we allow it. Only because we manipulate and control it and make it so. Where is the line between making your life happen, following your dreams, and making things happen for the sheer sense of safety, control and fear.

What would really happen if we just let go.

What is flow. Losing control or giving up? Maybe. Why is that so scary for so many. Has it always been this way? Have we always needed control to survive?

Questions hard to answer. I certainly don't have the answers. I don't know much. But I do know that the feeling of letting go is scary and freeing all at the same time.

What if there were no boundaries. No laws. What if there was no division between first class and coach and all the seats on the plane cost the same and everyone was equal.

Would it be chaos.

We place so much pride on being a nation of equal rights. I say yeah, right. The only thing equal in our country is that we have the right to choose.

That is the only real power we have in life. All other things are beyond us. You can choose to be afraid. Stay in your routine. Order the same food everyday. Get mad because someone takes your table. Or you can choose to be open to something new. Embrace the new view from a new table. Smile at those around you. Tip well because someone gave you good service. Stick up for your staff and believe in your people. Break the corporate rules so that the humane rules come first and become more important. Pay your staff more then $3.90 an hour so they can make a living that is fair.

Choice. Such a simple word isn't it.

Choice is power. Choice can create a world of beauty or destroy everything around us. Choice lies at every corner, in every room, in every molecule of air we breathe.

Some say they don't have a choice. Their circumstances are beyond their control. They say they are victims of life. To them I say maybe. But I doubt it.

Maybe if you are a child, perhaps, and have no rights to move out of your situation, but overall, every grown person has a choice.

We can learn to surrender our choices to others. Let others make our choices for us. Or we can choose to put ourselves in situations that take our rights away. Feed a stereotype; create a world according to others. Run around and be mad at everyone for everything. We can choose to destroy.

Or we can choose to live. Love. Breathe. Move. Create.

We can choose to ask for the same thing in our lives everyday, or we can choose something different.

Right now.

That woman taught me something that day. When she never returned, when anger took over and the feeling of being treated wrongly overcame her need for routine, I respected her more. I knew that she was off to new places. Something different. She was in a process of changing what was known for her and taking a risk and stepping into the unknown.

Maybe she just changed restaurants. But the view was different. The people were not the same. The experience was new.

Imagine the feeling of something new. Of something not being the same for just a moment. Close your eyes and imagine something you do everyday that is the same. It could be an aspect of your routine, the way you make your coffee, prepare your breakfast, or shower, or what you say to your loved one, kids, how you prepare for your day. Which route you take to work, how you treat you co- workers. Anything. Imagine it. See it well, feel what it feels like to you. The "same old, same old" in your life. Maybe how you have sex with your partner or spouse. The ordinary to it. The unexciting.

Now change it. The thing, person, position, phrase, way home, your coffee. What you say, the music you listen to.

What does it feel like now? What do you feel? Or can you not even imagine it at all.

Ask yourself what have you become so used to in life that you don't even notice it at all anymore. What person do you take so for granted that you didn't even bother imagining them as part of your routine.

Who did you think of the least? Say something to them today. Choose to see them today, smile at them. Let them know you see them. That they exist in this world.

Imagine how different your experience would be. And imagine how it would change the other persons experience too.

Routine.

We do it every day. All day. All the time. Sometimes we become spontaneous, and maybe we go and splurge on a new outfit, a hundred dollar pair of shoes, or we go on a dream vacation. I am asking you as my reader to look at the everyday choices. The everyday painting we paint for ourselves.

What colors do you choose. What pictures do you draw. Do you take chances.

It is your choice. Your power. Your dream that you live and create everyday and what you do with it lies in your own hands. No one else's.

You are not an unknown in this world. You are the known in your own world, the creator of your own dream. What you choose to dream is solely up to you.

Chapter 3

It has always amazed me how others judge each other. I knew a woman once who was a prostitute. She was young and beautiful. She had the best body I had ever seen, she would spend her time entertaining men for money.

She made a fortune. She had more money then anyone I knew. She sacrificed her body to make her money. She made more than many professional business people who had degrees from great schools, and spent years of their life learning, studying and brown nosing. She had made more money then all of them combined.

As she got older, the men paid less. Came around less. Her "clients" became more the type who had no choice but to pay because no other woman would give them the time of day, mostly because of how they looked.

Beauty is like an old painting. Everyone appreciates it and wonders at how incredible it must have looked once, with bright fresh colors, texture. How great it would be to restore such a work of art. But who has the time, money or interest in a no name painting not worth millions. Who cares about a work of art if it's not worth something to those buying it.

This woman was much like that old used painting. When one looked at her, they knew once she had been beautiful. Her body was still great, but tired. Used up. Some would say it was due to her profession, maybe disease, but mostly due to her job choice. "That is what you get when you are a prostitute!" they would all say. They would walk by her stick their noses up to her and never look back.

When the beauty faded the money stopped coming. Few will pay for a worn out prostitute. Everyone wants the fantasy they see on television and porn sites.

She hit some hard times, the money was gone and she was realizing all she had ever done with her life was sell herself. What skills did she have besides how to make a man orgasm and love her.

How is she any different then you or I? What makes her any different then anyone else? Nothing. We are all prostitutes. We all sell something of ourselves, our souls to survive. To provide, to make and have money. To live.

The only difference is what we choose to sell. Whether it is our bodies, our time, our interests, our dreams, even those we really love, desire, or want. We settle for something. We sell off our well being somehow to live the way we think we should, or how we should.

We offer ourselves up to the highest bidder. Who will take care of us the best, what partner should I choose so that I will have the best life, more money, a better stance, better looking kids. You name it; we are all prostitutes. We all are faded works of art.

How many times did you take a job because it was better money. Selling your true desires or dreams out for a better salary. Did you pick a prettier girlfriend because others would look up to you? Did you sell out on the uglier one even though you really liked her, because you worried too much about what others would think?

Did you turn away a lover because you thought another was a better choice? Abort a child because you thought your life would be easier without the responsibility of raising a child.

We do it all the time. We sell ourselves all the time. Everyday. That woman gave up her body for money. We give up our dreams for what makes more sense. For what makes everyone else happy. We let go of who we really are and what we really want in life so that we have what we believe we need. Be it money, fame, or title.

How many have sold out their true talents for others dreams of life. For the corporate vision. We are all prostitutes on some levels.

We have all sold our well being to something. Some of us even enjoy it. I always thought women who choose to be prostitutes got the best of both worlds, having sex all the time and making money. In ancient times prostitutes were known as priestesses.

Oh my, how times have changed.

This woman taught me much about myself. Watching her come in with her fake fur coat, pink heels and bright red lipstick. Having men buy her dinner before they got down to business afterward. I would watch her while others around me laughed. The looks of disgust being obvious, and I would wonder at who she really was underneath it all. Where did she come from, what was her name. After all she has a heart just like you or me. She is Human.

If I had not made the choice one day to ask her, I would never have known. If I had not let go of my judgments and never started a conversation with her whenever she came in by herself and sat at my table I would never have known and neither will any of us if we don't take the time to ask. To come closer to another human being and look past the clothes, choice of profession, lack of education, skin color or job ranking to see what lies beneath.

Take a risk and look deeper. You will find, when you do, some answers to all of these questions on your own.

And those answers are the only ones worth listening too.

But then again what do I know. I am just a woman in a mid life crisis. Questioning my life and everything in it. Maybe there is a reason everyone goes through this. Maybe it has to happen to wake us up and open our eyes.

Chapter 4

I always wondered what it would feel like if my husband and I were to split up and he would remarry first. I am so amazed at women who get thru this and seem to be ok.

I think they are either great actresses and can't deal with it at all, and just come off as being fine with it and break down when no one is looking. Or maybe they really are ok with it and have moved on.

I tend to think the first is more realistic then the second.

That exact thing happened to a good friend of mine awhile back, as well as my own mother. I have seen this side of life twice and both times it hasn't been pretty.

To me, that is what makes it beautiful. I have been able to see the real side of someone. Not the mask they put on so everyone thinks they are just fine.

Why is it such a need within our culture, especially our women, to appear to always be fine.

We aren't. So why fake it.

Why?

I knew a woman once whose husband remarried, he moved in with his new wife and bought a house together, and her children from another marriage.

When my friend turned 40, she had a huge party and all of her family came including their two kids they still shared custody with. The typical animosities that seem to always be between old wife and new, hung around like the stale scent of soured milk. She always said she was fine, even though her life was a mess since the divorce and she never admitted to anyone she regretted leaving him.

This day, perhaps because she had just turned forty, I had hung around afterward to help clean up.

It had been a wonderful day full of reconnection with family and friends. Her mother began to pull out old stuff, like pictures, you name it.

She pulled out her old wedding dress. We all just stared, and sat in our own space for a while. We all remembered that day.

Maybe it was the memory of all the dress brought back. Maybe it was the three beers she had drank. Maybe it was just the fact that we all sat around sharing our souls a bit after everyone had left. Maybe it was just the memories attached to all the little trinkets her mother had brought out for all to see.

Amazing what those closets are full of.

She stood up and took the dress and went into the bathroom. Changed and came out. It still fit. A feat not many women can claim. I know I couldn't!

I heard a car door slam outside, I looked out the window and to my surprise I saw the new wife's car. She was here to pick up the kids.

I saw a look in my friend's eye. A devilish grin filled her face and down the stairs she went.

Her mother and I got up and raced down behind her, we were yelling, "Don't do it! Don't do it!!

She went ahead and opened the door anyway.

As you can imagine the drama that unfolded did not disappoint anyone. We all had something to talk about for weeks.

But I saw something on my friend's face that day that I will never forget. It wasn't the devilish grin, or the decision to answer the door like that. It was the decision to act out in a way that made her heard. Even if it caused some drama, it helped her heal in some way.

It's amazing how things that come out of the closet can set us free. Free to move on, to let go. Maybe we need that one last stand between our old life and our new one before we can actually let a new life grow.

For her that moment was what it needed to be. For her it had to be a dramatic statement to the other woman. But it also showed a side of vulnerability.

Of hurt, leftover pain, that few people ever show others.

We are all so well armored. We walk around greeting everyone with armor on, vowing to never let another person see our "soft" side.

Our real selves stay hidden, and hidden well. Maybe we meet one person here or there that we can really be who we are with. But those people are few and far.

Showing the side of you that is vulnerable, outspoken, angry to others is not accepted in our culture. They get labeled. Judged.

I know well the pain of holding in anger. It creates a festering of emotion that poisons our bodies and souls. It makes you fat, lazy and afraid.

Letting it out might not be sociable acceptable, but the alternative is death.

That day when my friend did that I realized that life is just too short for niceties all the time. Sometimes you have to turn around and bite. So you can move on, let go and grow.

The many years I worked as a waitress, the socially acceptable thing made the company money. Show you care. Be polite. Serve and serve well. No matter how the customer treats you. They could be rude, demeaning and downright mean, and you would still have to say, "Yes sir".

I always wondered what would happen if I just snapped and told the customer how it is. What would happen?

Everyone there was so afraid of losing their job. So scared of the general manager, who had a reputation for firing people for whimsical reasons.

If you needed your job, and many of the people I worked with did, you kept your mouth shut. You kept your mouth shut to your manager, and to the rude customers you had to wait on hand and foot.

I wish I had the courage of my friend had that day. I wish I had spoken up for myself to the people who treated me wrongly all those years. I had once, and it didn't have a great ending.

So I never attempted it again. I chose to live my life like a wounded dog.

I always wondered what would be my "wedding dress" in that business. What would come out of my own closet, to push me over the edge so that I spoke up and gave my true feelings a voice. Showed my feelings and my vulnerability to others, said "Hello! You're being mean. Stop".

Stop.

Stop being mean.

I read an article today that broke my heart. A man had journeyed to Iraq as a Christian peacemaker. To work with the people there to try to come together some how. His intentions were good.

He was kidnapped, tortured and brutally murdered and his body left on the side of the road in a plastic bag. Like garbage.

What lies inside of us that makes us hate others. Why is this hatred so deep. So huge. It is like a force in this world that consumes us. Our families, lives, nations. Causes wars.

"In the name of God I kill you" a great and dear teacher of mine once said. Indeed.

When will it stop. When will the other person just stand up and say, enough. Please. Just stop.

Have we gone so far beyond going back that there is no turning back. Once we are armed with our words, fists, guns that's it. We just kill.

You see my divorced friend, the waitress, the Christian peacemaker, all have their own "wedding dresses" to wear. Points to make. They all reach a point where emotion takes over and they move. They choose. That choice brings them to their destiny. One step at a time. Every one of them has a choice. Yes, it may get you fired or even killed. But not choosing to wear it, not choosing to stand up for your true self, following your mind instead of your heart, following the rules even when it hurts you, will leave you in a much worse of a place. It leaves you dead inside.

If you could break one rule, any rule, what would it be? What risk would you take? What would be your "wedding dress"?

What emotions have you keep stuffed away in your closet for eons. What screams come when no one is looking. What masks do you take off at the end of the day when no one is looking. You are not alone. Everyone does it. Maybe that's the problem.

No one deals with others without those masks anymore.

If we did, perhaps no one would have to dance around in their wedding dress of choice, or be killed for trying to bring peace to an area so filled with hatred and war.

Hating is accepted. Showing emotion, vulnerability, your heart, is so feared and so very needed more today then ever.

My wedding dress was quitting my job one day. Finishing my shift, walking out and never looking back.

I said goodbye to my old life and welcomed a new one. I choose to speak up, be heard and reach out to others.

I believe in you. My reader. I believe that there is still hope out there in each and every one of us. Especially you. Right now reading these words.

There has to be. Even the murderers, the mean and rude customers, the General managers, the ex-wives, the bullies, the abusers, I know somewhere deep down inside under all the masks, the hate there is a spark of hope. Light. Maybe even love. No matter what you have done in life, you are still a human being who deserves to be whole.

Imagine if we took away all the labels. The deeds. The hurt and pain and believed in another human being. Believed in their heart to conquer all, to forgive and release all.

Imagine if we could shake hands with our enemies and embrace them as humans, like ourselves. With all our faults, anger, hate and just saw it for what it really is.

Armor. Armor to cover the hurt and pain.

Imagine a world with compassion. Imagine if we did not need the wedding dresses at all and could just show it without all the drama.

I challenge you to lay down your weapon of choice. Be it your words, emotions, put downs, judgments, labels, and just be who you are for one day. One moment. Make a choice.

Take your power.

Change your life.

Chapter 5

I noticed my pants were getting tighter a few years ago. I noticed and then tucked the thought carefully away so I wouldn't have to think about it, cry over it or do anything about it.

Maybe it would just disappear, go away and my thighs would magically shrink.

They didn't. They just got bigger, the message louder. My mind began to play an interesting game with my fat thighs. If I don't listen, then I can't hear you and I won't have to acknowledge anything you're telling me. Ha!

So my thighs came back and said oh yeah! Lets move on into your stomach, your behind, your neck, your face. Until the message is so loud and clear, you can't ignore me anymore.

You're Fat. Ha!

And I was. And still am. Here I am in my mid life. Overweight. So are half of my fellow Americans. We have that in common too.

So I go on about my day, doing what has to be done. With my lumps, sags and rolls. They follow me around like a well-behaved dog. I carry them like badge, a child or a heavy suitcase with all my belongings. Everyday. Everywhere.

My fat is my lover, my constant companion. I have a very typical relationship with it. Sometimes I love it, am indifferent to it or just plain old ignore it. You could even say I am married to it. My relationship with my fat is like that with any other being.

It has a life of its own.

Being a fat person is hard. I can pretend I don't care, nothing bothers me, or I'm just too busy to be bothered.

When I go shopping I hold my head high and go into the plus-size department and look for the latest style of "fatwear", as I choose to call it. What will make my behind look like a size 12 when it's really a 20! Come on. If that was the case the clothing companies would rule the world. And I would be sure to own stock.

I could probably squeeze it in if I try hard enough, but who really wants to see a fat person squeezed into three sizes too small. So I got over it and accepted my fat. I made a choice to give up.

I ate what I wanted and fed my fat everyday. I nurtured it, cared for it and hated it all at the same time. Kind of like my husband.

One day I wondered what my fat would look like if I cut a section off and looked at it. What does my fat look like. What is it made of. My sadness? Regrets? Anger? Hatred? Memories?

Layer on layer of forgotten and stored pain. Fat is my armor of choice. To keep others out. "Stay away!!" it says. And they do.

It worked for a long time. I went into a cave and wanted to hide. Get away from my life. I ate and ate and cried and cried. Of course, all to myself. I would never let someone see my vulnerabilities. That was just unheard of.

So instead I showed them my rolls. My double chins and my oversized elastic plus size pants.

And I faked just how happy of a person I was. I faked it just like an orgasm with my husband. Pretended my fat felt great.

I noticed when I was around thin people, other women especially, my size and false comfort with it, really offended them. Gosh, how could she be so happy and be so fat. That's disgusting. Their faces said it all.

I spent a lot of time exploring other things in my life, taking care of everyone else, especially my family. My body was not a priority. I wrote off my weight gain as superficial to care about. I was a deeper and more spiritual woman now; after all, I was a newfound member in the "new age" movement!

My body and pant size no longer mattered. And it didn't. So I believed my own lies.

I martyred myself. Accepted my size and pretended not to hear the comments, the laughter, or see the stares. I am a happy woman damn it!!

I even had myself convinced.

I had a conversation with my fat one day. I spent so much time with it so far, it's with me everyday, so why not get to know it. Isn't that just as important as knowing another person.

Making time to connect with another human being is what life is all about right? So why not do the same with myself and see what happens.

Have you ever done this? Talked to your own fat? Body? Or pain? Try it. Take what you like least about yourself and speak to it and listen to what it has to say. The most forgotten aspects of ourselves are our greatest teachers.

What is fat except an armor suit. A photo album of our past. Our fears. Our hidden from the world pain. It hides everything we don't want to feel. It takes care of all the uncomfortable times, moments, traumas and holds them safely for us.

We carry our own burdens. Our own trauma. The body records things at levels beyond our understanding and getting to those records and files buried deep is as hard as it is for a person who has never used a computer before in their life, to download a file. But who hasn't ever used a computer in this day and age.

So why should it be so hard too figure out what we are holding onto in terms of disease or fat.

One day someone close to me made a comment about my weight. Then another close person, then another. I was shocked.

Looking back it makes me laugh. Why on earth should it surprise me. Did I think if I didn't notice no one else would? Or if I just pretended it wasn't there it would go away, and if I didn't acknowledge it then it wouldn't exist? Yeah, nice try.

But once others began telling me I was fat, I could no longer hide, deny or run away anymore. They all pinned me down and made me look at myself.

What I saw staring back was scary.

Taking responsibility in life is hard. Owning up to what it is that one does to themselves is a lost art. Looking within is not encouraged in our culture anymore.

We would much rather hand over our lives, pain, and responsibility to someone else, a higher power, or our spouses and say do it for me, while we eat another Twinkie. Laugh at someone else, gossip about the fat woman in the restaurant ordering a diet coke with a double bacon cheeseburger.

No one wants to be bothered. No one wants someone close to tell them they are getting fat or not taking responsibility for what they are doing.

Why is it that we feel the need to be so politically correct these days.

Gosh don't offend anyone! They might sue. Or worse not like you. Or get everyone to hate you. There is a large business and much money to be made in that area. Someone offends you and off you go to a lawyer. You get a settlement and you go on.

What if they are right about you though. I was offended when my loved ones said I was fat. But I am fat.

I realized that day when the last of those closest to me said I was getting big, which is just another word for fat; I sat down and knew I could no longer run. Hide or deny what I was holding on to anymore.

The feelings below the surface needed to go. They needed to be set free. I needed to let go of what really had become my best friend, my lover, my husband. My fat had so many names. I had to let it go. Say goodbye, and let it die.

Sounds drastic maybe, but it was truth for me. My fat represented my past, and my fears, and all my pain, experience and holdings in life. I was tired of hiding. Tired of where I was at that point. I needed to mourn it, grieve it and bury it for good.

Cutting the cords to your parents is hard enough, cutting the cord to your own fat, or addiction, is very hard indeed.

I share my story, my vulnerability, my own weakness with you. I share my own faults, denials, embarrassments because it is these that make me human. And ordinary.

Eating, stuffing my emotions and my face were my addictions. What I took on to avoid fully living.

I realized that day as well, that I had a choice once again. Do I continue to walk around pretending I don't care, worrying about everyone else, and putting my own needs last. Stuffing how I really feel, or do I cry, yell, get mad, express, live. Do I choose to hate my body. Or love it? And in choosing love, how do I let go of the rest that no longer serves me.

My fat no longer served me. Perhaps it was like the moment when one knows without a doubt that they are with the wrong person, spouse, partner or job. That they can no longer spend another living, breathing moment where they are. The time has come to move. Change. Choose.

Seeing what it is that one has become, right there in that moment, and acknowledging it and taking responsibility to do something about it and stop being so damn afraid is the hardest thing I have ever done.

Perhaps in showing you, my dear reader, my own cracks and flaws it will help you understand me a bit more. See that I too, hurt, cry, hide and deny.

We have something in common. What is it in your own life or body that you deny. Refuse to see or look at. What is it that lies in the layers below the surface that run your life, hold your pain. What keeps you where you are.

Only you can look. Perhaps when others tell you one too many times that your getting "big", instead of picking up your weapons of mass destruction to blow your now new enemy out of the water, you can stop and look at what they are saying and ask them if perhaps they are right about you. Maybe they have in fact given you a great gift. A chance to cut away that layer of fat and look within, so you can finally see it for what it is and let it go, so you can move on and grow into a more whole person.

Chapter 6

I married my husband when I was young. I wanted to get out of my parents house at all costs and begin my life. I wanted someone to love me.

I wanted a husband.

Looking back now and looking at this from where I stand now, there is great sadness with my choices back then. I should've married for different reasons.

So much changes over the years. I had no ambition. I thought being married would magically make my life perfect. Better at least, then what I had at home. He was a good person. And he actually liked me.

I clung to him back then. He could provide for me, and he would take care of me. What more could a girl want in life?

I worked for years as a waitress to put my kids thru good schools, camps in the summertime.

What was left for me? Not much.

Except I could go to bed at night knowing I had done everything in my power to try to make everyone in my own home happy. Little did I realize then that always doing for everyone else leaves pain too.

My story is similar to many. Wake up. Make breakfast. Go to work. Come home. Make snack. Make dinner. Clean up. Go to bed. Maybe have sex with your spouse if you're lucky. Perhaps we have something in common here? Maybe we don't.

The routine leaves a void. A yearning that is very hard to ignore eventually. One day you look in the mirror and what stares back is old, tired, sad and most likely very, very angry.

It is very easy to understand why depression affects pretty much everyone at some point in their life. We have all felt some degree of depression, in some form or another. We do our best to run from it, hide from it, or lose ourselves in the addictions that help us deal with it, or not deal with it.

My kids are still young and growing. They are healthy and happy. What more is there to ask for? I don't know what their future will bring. I can spend every waking hour worrying, controlling, planning and it could still come out differently.

My sons play Little League. They love baseball. I enjoy going to their games. Watching them have fun, trying their best.

One year there was a boy on the team that was a great and naturally gifted player. Everyone loved him. Cheered him on. They knew he would help our team win. Winning is what most parents always want. I especially watched the dynamics of the games played off the field. I am sure many parents can relate.

The parents yelling, screaming, throwing things if their child gets out, or misses a catch.

The children just look bewildered. Some brush it off, others cry, some kids get mad storm off the field. It's no wonder most of them will have no interest in sports when they get older, or will drop out completely and turn to other games of choice. Or become such over achievers they spend their life trying so hard to be everything, fail and commit suicide.

How many of those T-Ball players will really become the next Arod. Maybe? It's always possible. You never know.

I watched this star player one day as he stood in short stop, trying to play both second and third base all at the same time. Trying to be everything.

His parents both came religiously to every game, coaching, yelling, screaming always at his shortcomings. Never at his strengths. The other parents just assumed he was so good because of how hard his parents pushed him.

This child had a beautiful smile. A big heart and always tried to help the other kids. I wonder if being pushed so hard would not only kill his interest in sports, but that heart of his as well. How much pain would he hold on too for never making his parents proud enough. Never being good enough in their eyes. Or being humiliated in front of his whole team, and the crowd.

What kind of mark does that leave? What kind of hole does that create and how will he choose to fill it? Cover it? Stuff it? Will he over achieve because deep down he just wants to make his parents happy.

Or will he give up completely and hate himself forever. Always struggling to love himself when he thought as a child he was never good enough.

The childhood pains leave such scars. Deep wounds. Layer on layer of self hate.

I wondered that day if the parents just stopped yelling, stopped swearing, and just enjoyed a good old afternoon of baseball, and if they stressed less on how horribly their son played, but instead on how great he tried, how that would change the course of his life forever.

My youngest son would finish his T-ball game and never know the score. "Did we win mom?" he would always ask me.

Most of the time I said yes even when he didn't. Just so he would smile, put his glove and bat away and spend the rest of the day happy, full of pride and he could laugh without disappointment.

Sometimes I told him the truth and said no. Because understanding that sometimes you win some and other times you lose some, is a part of life and either way life goes on.

You hang up your bat and you go on to other things.

These are the moments in my life that are great.

When I can just enjoy living. Watch a good game on a sunny afternoon, cheer when both teams make a good play, and know that no matter what, the balance of world power doesn't depend on the outcome, the score, or whether so and so caught that pop fly ball or not.

Those afternoons offered a change of routine every weekend. Something to look forward too. Something to go out and enjoy. I watched so many parents walk away from those games miserable, yelling at their kids, telling them how horribly they played, get in the car, you lose privileges for the day! They would shout. The child would cry, get mad, mostly just not understand.

What a tragedy. They had no choice in their treatment.

The choice each parent makes on how to react to their child changes their destiny. It changes their hearts.

As a parent do you choose power over? Or empowerment.

I was thankful for those moments. Those days with my boys. Watching them play. Having fun. Getting outside, running around, hot dogs after the games. I especially loved those!

You have a choice in life. The choices change everything around you. Including the lives of those you love most.

Those days I would go home and begin dinner, while they played outside and my husband would relax, or work.

One thing I knew for sure was, we were a family. Each of us has our own hearts, minds and sense of being. Each of us creates a life, a dream everyday. Each of us affects each other beyond words.

Stepping outside of the everyday routine, even for an afternoon T-Ball game, allowed something new to come in. Let some fresh air in and cleaned out that old and tired feeling to life. At least for a little while.

What is it that you do different from your everyday world. Do you enjoy it and relax into it? Or do you approach those breaks in routine with resentment. Control. Anger. Annoyance.

You can be like water, or you can be a wall.

Water flows around obstacles. Walls keep everything in or out, and whatever comes up against that wall hits and hits hard.

"Life is like baseball", someone once said to me. You can try to play all positions to make someone proud, and in the meantime give up all of who you are, spread yourself so thin you never focus on anything, or you can stay put, and master where you are at any given moment. Stand up and be fully present and grounded. Maybe you'll make a play? Maybe you won't.

However, for that moment, you are defined by your own standards. Your own dreams. Your own being. And not someone else's.

There is no greater accomplishment then that.

Chapter 7

How ignorant people can be sometimes. Some think the less we know the better. I like to believe in today's world we know the damage and threat in that concept of thinking.

Where is the fine line between taking care of ourselves and helping and caring for others.

I look around at times, as life passes by, and I watch. I watch the cars pass, the people walk by, their expressions, language, appearance and I just take it in.

What if we stripped it all away. What would be left. The clothing, skin color, gender. What if nothing separated us.

What if we took away the boundaries. The state lines, the nations, and just lived as one with each other. Sounds "Pollyanna" perhaps. Foolish some would say. Freedom of expression or the individuality of each person would be threatened, some would argue.

As a waitress, all those years, I learned to just watch, observe and just be as noninvasive as possible to allow the guests to enjoy their meal, without the intrusion of me.

I became very good at watching. I saw so many different types of people. Interactions between a wide range of personalities.

Black men and women would come in and I would watch so many servers doing all they could to not get them sat at their tables; by that I mean begging the hostess to not seat them in their sections. Myself included at times. I had just had one too many bad experiences waiting on black people. There is much to be said about reverse racism.

I hated waiting on white people just the same. That I must note. It isn't a race thing. Or a better tip thing. It's an observation in human treatment.

What will one person take, how much of it will they take and what's their breaking point?

Everyone has a breaking point. If pushed hard enough they will break. Some enjoy pushing so much, they tend to do it too anyone they can.

Push.

And push harder.

Abusers do it to those they abuse, and the victims tend to learn to do it to others, in subtle and not so subtle ways. The cycle continues and grows, out stretching until no one is left unaffected.

Like a ripple.

When you drop a stone into water, the ripples continue until they reach the shore. Everything within that fluid is affected, even if they don't know what hit the water.

Which stone do you pick up and throw. It is such a simple action and the affects are profound.

Making fun of a kid on your bus, or the girl in your class who is taller and bigger then everyone else, what words do you choose when you throw your stone.

The elderly person who walks slow or drives even slower. What stone do you throw at them. Is your stone full of love? Or hate?

Each has very different ripples, and even greater effects.

When a person cuts you off, perhaps even without intending too, you hunt them down to destroy them, give them the finger, maybe even cut them off back, perhaps you beat them to death when you finally hunt them down. Road Rage.

Revenge.

Such a life-taking concept.

Each stone is a gem of your own mind and intention. You color it, texturize it, fill it with your essence and you create it, you are God creating a force and throwing it out into the world.

Every time. In every way.

Those in the water are affected. Some maybe more then others, perhaps. Perhaps you hit a fish right on the head and kill it. Or you seriously wounded it and it is forever scarred. Or your stone landed in a bed of eggs and destroyed a whole generation yet to come. Or maybe it just gently fell and landed on the creek bed, and the ripples simply lifted or stirred the creatures below only for them to settle back down into their everyday way.

Either way you just keep walking and that stone never gets another thought from your mind, and yet you've affected an entire universe.

What would happen perhaps if we took the time to sit with that stone and look at it. See it. Make a choice of what to fill it with, how to throw it, or even if it should be thrown at all.

If we could fill a stone with just one word what would it be? Or a phrase? Or a feeling?

What if we knew everything in the water would be affected. Would we choose more carefully? Place it more carefully. Would we even care at all? Or would we throw it and say to hell with it all, I don't care either way. Maybe we even think our stone has no affect at all.

Words are like stones. The water is all around us. We throw stones everyday. We choose what to fill them with. We affect everything and everyone around us in all ways.

We are already connected, with no boundaries, no state lines, no political affiliations, no skin color. Nothing divides us. Not even our religious beliefs separate us. We are already all the same.

What divides us is our choice to care what stones we create, hold, mold, and throw. How we throw them, when and where, and which direction is our choice.

We all have the power to create and to destroy. We do it everyday already. With our children, family, co-workers, friends, lovers, spouses.

The waitress, the guest, the manager, the prostitute, the priest, the old woman who lives next store, the teenager with a hundred piercing, the woman who lives in a village in Africa, the Muslim, Christian, Jew, Catholic, all have the power within to create and destroy.

And that power to do so is the same within each and every living human being. It sees no difference between any of us.

The power is not racist, and it sees no lines, no separation, and it lives in every living being on earth.

That power does not believe in one way, my way, no other way. It believes in all ways and knows that you right now can redirect, change it and use it to create life, love and bring peace into your own world, and in doing so you change your stone, your ripple and you change the world.

It believes in you. You just have to believe in yourself.

The way the world is affected is all up to you. Not the groups, corporations, presidents, churches. Just you and your stone.

But again what do I know? I'm just a retired waitress and a mother of two. A Master of peanut butter and jelly sandwiches.

Chapter 8

So how are you at this point? We have shared some time together and I must take a moment to say thank you for sitting awhile and listening. I have never been one to be heard much. Being seen and not heard has helped me make better tips all my life. It became a way of life in a way.

However, sitting here talking with you about life, things in it, asking questions to stir the mind a bit, has helped me. For that I say "Thank you" to you. We may never see each other in person, but you have helped me feel heard. You have helped me grow in a way.

You may not agree with all I've said so far, and that is ok. I am not here to change anyone's mind. I am just here to sit and share a bit of my life, the stories in it, and maybe a bit of wisdom I may have found along the way.

Take what you will and leave the rest. But I feel compelled to thank you as my reader for staying and sharing with me. You are indeed helping me heal in a way.

That is what it is all about I think. As I look around at my life at this point, and what I have and have not done with it. I feel the affects of my own choices and wounds that I have had inflicted and also caused to others along the way. If I can't learn from them, then what is the point?

You are a complete stranger, as am I, and we have shared something.

To me, that is the most beautiful thing I could ever do with my human life. We both come from different places. We both have such different ways of seeing, thinking and being, and yet there is something that has kept you reading this far. You haven't shut the book, put it down and walked away. You haven't felt so angry at my words, thoughts or insights that you closed the book and yourself and walked away.

Something has kept you here. You have chosen to keep the book and yourself open.

I don't pretend to know all the answers. Or to understand everything. But I do believe in you. I believe that you want love, peace, joy and connection in your life versus hate, anger, and separation.

That is perhaps, what has kept you here with me, and together our listening, sharing with each other, believing in each other, we can change our lives, and our world.

Or not.

Either way, whether we change the world, or just laugh and maybe even cry together, then it has all been worth it.

To you my dear reader I say thank you for being on this journey with me and you deserve your own chapter.

Chapter 9

I grew up believing that being born a woman was a life sentence at non-accomplishment, low wages and even lower expectations. I had one mission and one mission only according to those who raised me. Get married. Get pregnant. That will be your life. That's the only goal you have, oh yeah and finish high school, turn 18 and get out of the house. If my parents accomplished that with me, then they have raised me well in their eyes.

That was my life mission since I could remember. According to everyone else that's all I could hope for, and at best maybe I would marry someone with money and have an even better life then what my own parents had together. Being happy. Well, if you had that then you really lucked out. If you had all of it, then that was all the world could give me, and all I should expect from it.

I was sentenced, and condemned at birth because I have a vagina.

The reinforcement I got throughout my life, from parents, teachers, even other women! Made it all a self-actualized dream. A self-fulfilling prophecy.

I wonder what it would have been like if they told me when I was born that I would be President of the United States, and that's just they way it is. Accept it. How different my life would be.

No one ever told me I was worth something, that I would be great. That I would and could accomplish something with my life and I could make a lot of money doing whatever I wanted. That I mattered.

I was a girl. All I had to worry about in life was being pretty enough to attract a man.

And sure enough that's all I did. Worry about being pretty enough to attract a man. So I could get married, have children and love it.

Well here I am. And life tells me there is a whole lot more out there for me than just the hopes of having a great husband. Being a mother and going to bed at night loving it.

Sure I love parts of it. At times it is rewarding. But when I sleep at night I get thirsty. A thirst that is not easily quenched by waking up and making breakfast, packing lunches, doing laundry and then going to work and serving sandwiches and coffee.

I fulfilled that destiny in my life, since it was the only one I was given or believed I had. I accepted what others told me and I believed it. And so then it came true.

Being in a marriage is interesting. The dynamics are unique. My husband is a "man's man". All other men that aren't "men's men" are gay. His general attitudes towards women are like that of most men in his family or even his generation: women are here to serve.

His philosophy on women is common, and many other men follow the herd with this one.

Women should serve, serve well and like it. Give up all dreams, and always be there for everyone else. And love it.

If this was true, and true to the betterment of all, why is it then when most women conform to this ideal, are they, the men, so miserable? The women, so miserable?

The men begin to get bored. And suddenly do you not only have to be the family waitress, but now the porn star goddess he stares at on the Internet when no one is looking.

A woman has to BE whatever it is that a man wants, whenever he wants it.

She has to shape shift into whatever is wanted at any given moment in time. One minute cooking up a delicious home cooked meal, the next, stripping down to a G-string and sliding down a pole. Then she has to change once again, and clean the house.

This talent is never seen, acknowledged or paid for.

Is the woman property then? Did he buy her when the wedding vows were exchanged? Is the priest at the church where they married really a real estate agent in disguise?

Who owns a woman, if she has no interest in owning herself.

If I had been raised differently and believed in myself, my mind would've seen the world differently. I would've created a different life for myself. It took me a great many years to realize I was allowing others to taint my sunglasses their color of choice. I had to take off the glasses altogether, choose a new pair and color it my own color.

Perception is a funny thing. We all throw our own stones, but we also create them too. When you're walking along the sidewalk and you bend over and pick up a rock, it is you who has created that rock in the first place.

Not only are you responsible for what you fill that rock with, where you throw it and what happens because of it, you created the rock to begin with.

How? By choosing to believe the rock exists in the first place.

I believed that I could accomplish nothing more in my life then to be a pretty wife for someone and that was my rock. I created that rock. Then I filled that rock with what I wanted and then I threw it.

It's kind of like fishing. You pick your pole. Put your bait of choice on it and you throw it out into the water. You are trying to attract a fish.

You attract in life what you believe. Your mind is an endless, vast space. Why don't we know much about it? Why don't we use more of it? Or even know how to access far regions of it?

I have no answers for those questions. But they are worth pondering.

I do know that the mind births what we believe to be true. In a way it is a womb. Where all life comes from. Where all life is designed, created and given form.

Perhaps that is why we all have a different perception of the world around us, because we are all giving birth to our own creations all the time. My creation may not look like yours, or even be close to yours, but it is still a creation. It still exists.

Some people have similar perceptions; they create similar stones to throw together as a couple, a group or an organization. Perhaps those similar perceptions are like brothers and sisters, they look related, but still not quite the same. Each unique, different, special and very real.

You can allow others to choose which rocks you will create, tell you where to throw them. Or you can take responsibility for your own creations, and decide for yourself.

The mind is a womb. It births our world around us. We all have a mind; therefore we all have a womb.

Therefore, in my opinion we are all female.

Chapter 10

We as a human race do not have the luxury of time anymore. Our survival as a species is at stake, and it is evident everywhere.

The ancient teachings all over the world, in every culture, keep their teachings encoded, their sacred mystery teachings only available to a select few, or those who can figure it out on their own, who can read through the printed word and find the message carefully hidden between what is actually written. Or to those with large checkbooks who can afford the truth for sale.

We no longer have enough time to figure out the mystery of those who have come before us. We have to understand the human mind and its makings now.

The truth has to be given to each and everyone of us, so that we can all grow, change and begin to take responsibility now, before we commit suicide collectively as a species.

It is no longer about chasing terrorists thru the deserts of the Arab world, or starting another war with another country, it is bigger then all of it. We have to find an end to the war within ourselves before the war without will end.

Hating each other is no longer an option, being intolerant to each others differences is no longer relevant, dealing with life, just getting thru living life, is no longer an option.

We have to change our lives. And we have to change them NOW.

We all make choices everyday. We make decisions over everything. It is no longer something to just sit around a table or on a talk show and just talk about, we have to DO it.

We have to choose. Every moment, of every day, do we choose life and creation in all we do? Or death and destruction?

Is your choice life giving? Or life taking?

It won't work if you just change at one level or another, or about making someone else do something, or changing someone else's mind.

It is about changing YOUR OWN mind.

It is about accepting that you are in fact a creator. You have the power of the original source within you and you have to own it, love it and then choose how you will use it.

Our species will one day be like that of the dinosaurs. Gone. Extinct. Either by our own means or by nature's.

What we do while we are here is really up to us. We can spend our days arguing about who's right or who's wrong, who's better or worse, who has the right to this or that, who deserves more or less, who is prettier or uglier, who is a better actress or actor, what to wear or not to wear, to love their husbands, lovers, partners or not, who has the better God, who has more of a right to oil, or land, or money. But what it comes down to is who doesn't have the right?

We all have the right. We all deserve to be seen, heard, believed. We all have the right to abundance, to an opinion, to a belief.

Where are our voices? Where are our listeners? If no one listens, why bother speaking.

Chicken Little said the sky is falling, and no one believed him. But the sky did indeed eventually fall.

We all have ears. We have to use them. Listen to those around us. Listen to our own heart.

What is it saying?

Trust is a hard thing for everyone. It was for me for most of my life. I still struggle with it. When you are told to never trust anyone, in large and subtle ways, you don't.

When your trust has been betrayed once, or many times, you turn trust off like a light switch. You become paranoid. All of us are paranoid in one way or another.

Never trusting your spouses, co-workers, bosses, governments, people of other faiths. Someone is always trying to get you, get over on you, or take what you have. Right?

So we keep everyone and everything out, lock our doors, bar our windows and our hearts.

We put up signs saying, "Keep Out"

And they do, and they get more and more suspicious of you in return. Why do they want to keep me out? They must be doing something wrong.

A vicious cycle begins.

Threats, suspicions, worries, fears. All create a world of their own. World leaders don't rule the world, fear does.

We worry about terrorists taking over. Its not just terrorists we should worry about, its our own fear and distrust in others we should be spending billions and billions of dollars on.

Enough of the games.

Lay down the weapons, not just the guns, or nerve gas, but the fear. The hate. The judgment. The crusade. You can't change anyone except yourself.

Take a look around, really look around, watch the nightly news, listen to the wind. Start to think for yourself. Start to listen to your own words, feelings, and heart.

Believe in yourself.

Chapter 11

In the last few weeks in my career of waiting tables, I ran into a woman I had not seen for over 15 years.

We exchanged numbers and I called her and we got together. Her life had changed drastically, as had mine; 15 years can't really ever go by without drastically changing you in some way.

She was a born again Christian. Perhaps it was where I was at in my own midlife crisis at this point, but we sat and talked for four hours, where as years before I would've got up and left.

"You're not converting me!!" I would've claimed and stormed out. "I know your kind!" I would've said to her years ago.

I made a choice right then and there to just go with it. I chose to just listen.

I walked away that day, not feeling like I had been put through a ringer of judgment, damnation and the push to conform. I walked away clear, sure of who I am, and proud of myself for sitting with her, letting her speak her own passion, her own beliefs, and not making fun of them or judging them.

I choose to see the beauty of our differences, our similarities and of course, that she is also a human on the path of life, trying to do what I do, just make sense of it all.

When I told others that I had spent four hours with a born again Christian, the reaction was varied. Some rolled their eyes and laughed, others worried that I wasn't ok; some felt pity for me.

No one just said, "So? What did you have for lunch?" If she had been a Muslim. A Jew. A Shaman. A Mystic. A politician. Would my experience have changed? Would others' responses?

If you can stand in your own circle, know yourself, love who you are, then no-ones' beliefs will ever hurt you, betray you, because they don't define you. You define yourself.

I accepted her literature, and let her pray for me when I left. We could all use a little blessing in our lives; does it really matter where it comes from?

If we are indeed all the same, then the dress up costumes we choose to decorate our lives with don't really matter. What matters is that we know they are just that, costumes.

Costumes that we choose to wear and be seen in, but underneath it all we are the same.

My oldest son once asked me if our hearts all looked the same, even if we didn't. "Yes they do." I answered. Then he asked me "Then why do we all look different?"

I said, "Because we are all unique and special." He was ok with that answer and just moved on.

Imagine if our leaders around the world were just ok with that answer, and just moved on.

The Egyptians understood that the face was indeed the only thing that truly made us different. For them each face was how the Gods in the afterlife recognized you.

Each face showed your own individuality in the sea of many, yours was like no one else's. Without it no one would know who you are.

Your mind and what you create is like no one else's, unless you let it be. Your choices belong to you and no one else. You may think you are entangled and your arms and legs are tied to your situation, your boss, job, spouse, but it is only because you haven't believed you can choose differently. Or you're afraid of something.

I believe in you. I believe that under whatever costumes you wear, you have a heart and it beats. I believe in your power. I believe in your voice.

I believe that you will believe in yourself and that your life will change when you let it, no matter what exists around you today. I believe in your beauty as a fellow human being.

Chapter 12

This book has been my rock. I decided to quit my job one day, to take control of my life and trust what would come. I had to believe in myself, stop choosing fear and trust in myself and in my own power.

I had to let go of all the old wiring, and rewire myself. It was a choice and it happened in a split second. I was the one who had to do it. I was the one who could choose for myself, to love life, instead of fearing it and hating it. I changed my beliefs about myself and then my world changed around me because I listened to my own heart. I believed that my life could change, and it did.

I had spent my entire life running from pain and every decision I made back then was based on that sole principle. It ruled my life. Finally one day I decided to stop, to change directions and move differently with different intent. I decided to become a "pleasure" seeker.

By that I mean, I decided to enjoy life and all it is. Good, bad and ugly. Because without it how boring would it all be. If everything is perfect all around me, how would I learn.

What I had to do that day was make a decision to become a decision maker, a choice taker. I had to choose responsibility for actions, choices, desires and myself. I had to take a risk and throw out my everyday ordinary rules and step out into life. I had to stop taking myself so seriously and start laughing. I had to choose to be a human being.

I had to forgive everyone in my life that had hurt me. Which I did. I could honestly say I forgave them completely, every single one. I hope someday those I hurt along the way, will do the same.

When I decided to stop being a waitress, I decided to take up real estate and become an agent. What

I soon realized was that like waitresses, real estate agents are all grouped into a gigantic hole called "all the same", but once again I had to find the humor in the bigger picture of it all, and know whether I am selling burgers and fries, homes or a book, it all comes down to the same thing either way. Its not what you sell in life, or what you make off the interaction, its how you live in that interaction and how you choose to be.

Most importantly, and really all that ever will matter on any level, is how you treat the other person you are interacting with. No matter who it is, a lover, a spouse, a child, a stranger, a waitress, a real estate agent, a potential client or a bum on the street. You treat them the same. No matter what color, race, religion, gender. No matter what they have done in their life, no matter what choices they have made thus far, because you could very well change their life, by simply seeing them, hearing them, listening to them.

You may never even know it, but with that simple act and in that very instant, you could change someone's life, and if and how you approach that moment, whether it be with love, joy and hope, or with hate, judgment and fear. You have not only changed their world, but also your own.

It starts with each of us, not by throwing the politicians you don't agree with out of office, it starts by changing yourself. After all, that's all you really have complete control over.

I wonder what makes someone hate someone else, when they have never even interacted with them. It happens all the time. "I don't like her", or "I hate real estate agents, they are all the same." Is it a bad experience with one along the way that made someone decide that? What made them choose to group people together based on one interaction. What makes a man think is he superior to a woman. Or a General Manager better then any employee below him.

Perception.

What is this thing called perception anyway. Is it a disease? Can you catch it?

AIDS won't destroy the world; neither will the terrorists, or the bird flu, however perception will. We have already caught it like a sexually transmitted disease, and it spreads with everyone we come in contact with and has already infected the world. You are infected right now where you sit.

The good news is that perception has a cure, and you don't have to pay for it, get a prescription and help make a drug company billions of dollars in order to get it, or have a great HMO. You just have to choose it. You already have the cure within you.

Perception can be a deadly, life taking, disfiguring disease, or it can be a beautiful act of conception. A creation of a new world. Just like that, it's just that simple.

Imagine a cure that can't be charged for. Now that would throw the balance of world power off wouldn't it.

You want real change in your world? Then change yourself first, and care about everyone no matter who they are.

How we choose to perceive is the only true right we all share as human beings. Perception is the only parcel of land we ever truly own outright. When all the laws of the world are gone and it's just you and I sitting at a table facing each other, it is the only thing we have left. It is the only thing that sits between us on the table, whether it is a dinner table, or a boardroom table.

Some may say you need perception to survive. That like attracts like.

Like the billions of endless amounts of stars above our heads every night, imagine each star represents one entire world of perception, like grouped with like. Which one will you choose to live on, or take energy from. It is your own choice and your own making, and that choice determines your entire life experience.

That is what I have discovered life is all about so far. Enjoying everyone I interact with, and when someone comes along and tries to make that interaction full of life-destroying perception, I see it for what it is, ignorance and disease, and I walk away. In my mind

I thank them for showing me once again how simple it all really is, because without them I wouldn't know the difference, nor would I have a choice to make, and choice is power.

So here I am, learning how to sell real estate, writing and following my own dreams, making my own choices. What I am mostly grateful is for you, my reader, because without you there would be no interaction, no chance to choose, no one to listen. Because of you, I am no longer an unknown. My voice has been heard. My thirst quenched. My crisis is over.

I searched for something and I found it. I found it in myself, and in you. Thank you for sharing the journey with me.

The End.

Or is it? What about the marriage? The kids? The everyday? What does "The End" really mean? What happens now.

Thru my journey with writing this book, putting my thoughts to paper, things began to change in my life. Truly change. I had to really walk the walk. Not just say it all on paper, tell you, the reader, how to do it. I had to DO IT too.

So was my crisis really over? Or is it just over within the context of our time together in the "story". What happens when you close the cover and I type "The End".

Do I go back to my once miserable life.... "preaching" the way, or do I do it too. Do you? Who does?

So many times I have read books, enjoyed my time while they lived within my life, as I call it. And when I was done I put them on the shelf, and walked away. Back to my real life. Story over.

Very few books have ever stuck with me for a long time. Their words blend in with the sounds and happenings of the everyday world. Unless they are studied religiously forever.

Some stories you remember, usually the ones full of sex, drama or murder and violence, because that describes our collective world.

You could close this book, walk away and continue on with your world, your life and I would never know, nor would you know if I did, or didn't.

I can tell you that working on this book motivated me. I began to change how I treated myself. I still took care of those in my life, but I began to see just how neglected I had been to myself, and I also began to see how neglected I was in my marriage.

On the outside, physically my life appears fine, and others envy the things my husband provides for me. But what he didn't provide was attention, affection and support in all other areas OTHER then physical, by that I mean he paid the bills, bought the cars, the houses, the businesses. But they were always in his name, all his. Never ours.

The word "ours" did not exist in our world together. Ever. Except for our children. He couldn't find a way to say they were solely his.

I didn't know any better all those years. I just accepted my life as is. Grateful he was there to provide and save me. The rest I could do without, I mean how important are they really anyway! Who needs affection, and love when you have a new home, a car that is paid for? Mind you he always had the new cars and I always had the paid-for station wagon. What took me so long to wake up to this? Did I know it at a level way below conscious understanding?

Of course I did; we all do. Admitting it is a whole other story.

When I took a risk and left being a waitress, I began to write, and doors opened for me. I also decided to take a real estate course so I could change my income. What I got out of that class mostly, however, was what my rights are. I realized how I had none according to the way the legal documents, deeds and titles had all been set up by my husband. I realized how little I knew about life.

I began to question my financial situation between my husband and I, and realized I had nothing to stand on legally if we ever got divorced. He had set it up that way, and I had no idea.

I just trusted what he said to me. I made a choice and I began to make some calls. I began to start asking questions, looking at filed away, very quickly I might add, financial statements. What I found was astonishing.

Taking that real estate course not only gave me a license, but it gave me a clue.

Pay attention. Know what your rights are, and also know those handwritten numbers with another woman's name on it is never work related. Ever.

My point here isn't the drama of my own situation, but to help other people, women especially, to know better.

Even if your marriage is perfect, know where you stand legally. Your husbands or partners do! You can only pretend it doesn't bother you for so long before it eats away at you or finds its way into your own layers of fat. Or soul.

Knowledge is power and it gives you more choices. It is just up to you to act on them.

This is a common dirty secret I think. Women go about their life, and secretly die inside and no one knows, because on the outside we all look perfect, or we appear at least ok.

In my fat lies loneliness. Neglected by my husband, among many other things. Am I saying skinny people have no problems? Absolutely not. Their pain just hides somewhere else. Pain can fit into any sized space.

As I finish this book, these last few thoughts, I sit in a diner with my laptop. Alone. Being waited on by a waitress. I have now become the guest. She's probably looking at me sitting here with my laptop out, during a busy lunch and thinking "great there goes my table for the whole day!", or maybe she isn't. I used too think that. I used to think a lot of things.

Regardless, however, I will leave her a good tip and she will go on with her day. I will go on with my life; maybe I will get a divorce? Maybe I won't, but I know too much now for my marriage to ever be the same again. I believe in myself too much now for my life to ever be the same again.

Funny how things come full circle in life.

I am not going to write the words "the end" because I don't believe in them. I think the road goes on forever indefinitely, and all that matters is that you just keep moving, know what direction your heading in, and decide which way to go when you come to a crossroads. As long as a road isn't one way, you have a choice. And you have power.

Most important is that YOU make the choice, and not allow it to be made for you.

Remember to be nice to those you meet along the way, see them, hear them, discern what is right for you, and educate yourself.

And please don't forget to tip your server well; after all they are unknowns too.

Some people go out and buy a big red fancy sports car during their mid life crisis's. I choose a trip to Egypt as my sports car. I wonder if I will make that journey there as a single woman. Maybe I will share that journey as well someday. I wonder if I will even come back.

I wonder a lot of things still, but they don't seem as big and frightening anymore. They seem more like possibilities. I like the sound of that better anyway.

All the choices in life, and of all the possibilities, imagine how infinite our power really is as a human being, as a race.

I choose to be like the wind. A warm west wind that brings with it a warm touch, a gentle scent and the truth of transition.

I look around at my own life and know no matter where I go from here my life belongs to me. I know I belong to myself and no one else. That the pain I have lived through has indeed been for a reason. I don't blame anyone else anymore. My crisis for now is over. I seem to have circled my own truth, like a wolf circling prey, I stalked it and hunted it so I could feed on it and keep living. I circled my own truth, claimed it and now I forever own it.